GIN
ON THE
ROX

VS GRIFFIN

PGM
INCORPORATED

GIN ON THE ROX

Printed in the United States of America

PGM, Inc LLC Publishing, 2020

ISBN 978-1-7349445-3-2

PGM, Inc Publishing
www.pgmincllc.com

DISCLAIMER

First and foremost, just for clarity. I am and will forever be a follower of Jesus Christ. There are some triggering moments in this book that while once traumatic for me, I hope will be cathartic and healing for someone else. This book is by no means a solicitation to change anyone's beliefs. If you do, then I celebrate with you, brother, or sister. However, if you do not, I still celebrate with you and hope as well as pray that you did receive what I intended and that is … hope. This book is about my life. Everything I have celebrated, everything I have survived and how God was there from the very beginning. My goal is to show whoever needs to know that you will experience challenging situations and that you also can make it through the bad times. Do not give up, ever! I made it through and still make it through... YOU CAN TOO! I will also be speaking candidly and very matter of fact in regard to some triggering information. Please do not take it as me being callous, I have arrived at a certain level of acceptance and my past has no power over me. It is my hope that someone finds inspiration, healing & hope.

Also, I was adopted by my maternal grandmother. For the context of this book, I am going to use correct titles based on the biological makeup of things except for my parents. I will not disrespect everything they went through to raise me so they will always be referred to as Momma & Daddy.

Names have been changed for privacy reasons.

Peace, love, light, and blessings in Jesus Christ name. 💜

"So glad I made it, I made it through.

In spite of the storm and rain, heartache, and pain,

I'm still alive declaring I made it through.

See, I didn't lose.

Experienced loss at a major cost,

but I never lost faith in you.

So, if you see me cry, it's just a sign that I'm still alive.

I've got some scars, but I'm still alive.

In spite of calamity, He still has a plan for me

and it's working for my good.

It's building my testimony!"

Marvin Sapp, *My Testimony*

In Loving Memory of:

Sencire V. Griffin-Horton

*

Virginia Marshall Pennie Griffin

*

Prentice O. Pennie

*

Cecilia Marie Austin the "Yellow Bandit"

Table of Contents

Foreword

By

Michel Roy

Edited by

Junious King

Love is free and so are we when we live our lives as we were designed by our creator. We are simple, yet complex expressions of love. It is through life experience that we begin to seek the approval of others and forget who we are and close ourselves off to love. This book is about freedom as humans and freedom from judgment, so let's discuss this thing, judgment. Judgment is defined by Webster in many ways- the process of forming an opinion or evaluation by discerning and comparing, an opinion or estimate so formed, a formal utterance of an authoritative opinion, a formal decision given by a court, and as a divine sentence or decision by God. As human beings we begin our lives free from the constraints of judgment and the opinions of others, but as we grow, we come to realize that here in this place under our sun that judgment is handed out freely and based on little more than a cursory glance by a stranger. We also learn very quickly to judge ourselves, very harshly based on those judgments that have been handed to us by others. I'm no different. I have spent years judging myself based on what someone told me or what dreadful thing I told myself when I wasn't feeling well. When my friend Virginia asked me to take part in this project, I was excited and honored that she thought so much of my writing skills. I have always wanted to be published on some level, but I had my reasons for never really affirming that I wanted to be a writer. I thought I could possibly be an editor at one point, but with my lack of attention to detail and my inability to focus for prolonged periods of time stopped me from pursuing that endeavor. I was still judging myself, not based on my skills as a writer or by the validity of what I had to say - but based on my previous inability to accomplish tasks and not being able to see myself for who I am now, in this moment.

I often see people using their ability to see, hear, and feel to place judgments on themselves and others, the same way I had done for most of my life. We look at our neighbors and wonder why they don't spend more time to cultivate their yards or why they let their children behave in a way we might find reckless, because we would never behave that way. It seems we have developed a way of life that is based primarily on the judgment of others, based on what we've decided personally to be unacceptable or acceptable from our egos. The ego is the king of make believe and imagination, in that it will help to deceive you and aid in your deception of others. It's our mask here; it's what we put on when we're ready to go into society. The same people who judge others too harshly for their parenting styles or for how they carry themselves in society are the same people with the most shame. You might wonder how I can make an inference like that about such a large group of people, well, it's because I used to be one. I had so many things I wanted to be perfect in my life, that instead of taking the time to fix what I could about myself and my situation, I just used that energy to practice bitterness and judgment from my seat. It wasn't until I started my own journey to heal that I became aware of how this behavior was affecting me, and what it was doing to my family. I am grateful for that time in my life, as it is the basis for my coaching program SMART LOVE, where I teach people to unlock and unblock themselves to live a purpose driven life. I learned incredibly early on that I was wrong to judge others the way I had been, as we are all healing here. That's the purpose of this experience, to heal and to awaken your ego to the mission of your soul.

Walking through life as the self-appointed Honorable judge Ms. Roy was not working for me, and I'm fairly certain that on some level you understand that being a judgmental person isn't working for you, either. You probably feel like you aren't successful and most of the things you try to achieve are met with some sort of blockage: That's because of the standard you have set for yourself! You're judging yourself just as harshly - if not more harshly than you're judging others. You see, when we decide there is only one "right" way to live here, we make it our business to keep ourselves hostage in that space. It's not a conscious thing; you don't realize that you're doing it. It's not your "intention" to hold yourself captive by the bounds of this society or the things you learned growing up with a family who probably did the best they could, but it's happening. Consider some of the things you really like to do and note which of those things make you feel shame when you think of someone else commenting on your desire to create art, or to dance, or to write, or even to participate in activities that seem reckless or juvenile. Those are your judgments against yourself and are likely the same things you make negative comments to others about when you see them enjoying themselves or their lives without a care for what the rest of the world thinks. The truth is, you're jealous of them because you also want to be free, and since I'm being honest, you can be. If you allow it.

Judgment is a great skill to have, as it's something we all possess the ability to do with great ease. We should use it in the way it was designed by our creator. In the Tarot there are two ways we see judgment: with the Judgement card and the Justice card. Neither of these cards mention placing judgment on others, however, they both mention reaching to your higher self for direction in times when you need to seek truth, and when it's time to level up. Coincidentally, it has been decided by The Universe that we are not the ones who make the judgments here, we are but expressions of God seeking to balance our dark and light parts to become whole. Due to the interesting nature of this gift, it is no surprise that we continue to misuse it. If used correctly, judgment can level up your entire experience and change your life for the better. It all boils down to the way you use it. If I want to discern something, then I am naturally using judgment - and this is what I mean when I say there is a way to do it- discernment is for your benefit. It's how you determine whether or not you should take next steps, and how you know if what you've been doing is really serving you and if those actions are for your greatest good. Without it we would all be lost; it's one of our God given gifts and we are not using it for its intended purpose.

Living a life of internal discernment versus one of external judgment opens you up to so many possibilities: it's the way those of us who are brave enough to tell our stories decide how and when to do it. If we were concerned about judgment, we would not tell the truth of how we came from the dark to the light, or how we knew when we were wrong and when we were doing right. There's a gift there, in being free. It allows you to become the person you were meant to be. We did not come here to this earth to live mediocre lives that are built on "whether or not" you should do something, or "you should say this or that because if you do people might think you are one of those people." Whatever that means… What does it mean to be one of those people? I think for some, it means to be the type of person who has no decorum or sense of responsibility to the rest of us; to live wild and so recklessly. The fact of the matter is this: when you decide that you no longer care what this world thinks of you, you seek to rise based on the feeling of exhaustion that builds from trying to keep up with the Joneses and to be polished and seen as the image of perfection you allow yourself to see a different view. Life isn't meant to be so constricting, and when you give yourself permission to live it without bounds you also come to know love that you haven't been exposed to, living in the way of judgment. When you rise to your truest form and your best self, you take all the dreams and desires you've ever had off the shelf; you let more love in and you let more love out and you begin to understand what humanity is really all about. You're able to extend grace to others and to forgive your sisters and brothers for what they've done here, and for the way all those things made you feel. I know some people don't agree with forgiveness, but it's part of the magic for me. The space you create in yourself when you stop holding on to bitterness, ego constrictions and judgment is filled with light. That's how you make it here, with discernment and the light of the world inside of you. As I said in the beginning, only God (the Creator) can judge us, and we are all connected to that entity. Who we are now are only pieces of Him.

I hope you enjoy this book and that you learn something from the pages within. Thank you for reading this and congratulations to my friend, Gin.

Dear Mama...

"I reminisce on the stress I caused; it was hell
Hugging on my mama from a jail cell"

- Tupac Amaru Shakur

Life can be complicatedly funny sometimes. This book has changed more times than my major in college. Initially it was a sequel to my debut novel *Phoenix Rising* but, and stay with me here, my heart was not going in that direction. Then, the book changed to an autobiography, and I quickly scratched that idea simply because I did not want to deal with the legalities that were sure to arise. So, one night as I was rocking my newborn daughter to sleep, a hashtag that I used on many petty and shady social media posts came to mind. "Judge Ya Mammy."

This hashtag was something I started saying when I posted something controversial or unpopular in opinion. That lead me to the new direction that this book would take which is still discussing my life but also my unorthodox views and unpopular opinions in regard to my Faith, parenting style and just general ideologies. So, basically a memoir of sorts. There is no chronological order to this book. This also is not a tell all. It is my reflective view of the major tribulations I have overcome as well as the unexplained joys along the way. Basically, Gin... on the rox. Unfiltered. Unashamed. Unveiled.

****

May 27, 1982, I was born at Jefferson Davis hospital in Houston, Texas and given the name Virginia Pennie. My birth mother whom I will refer to as "Lynn" named me after her mother (my maternal grandmother, who we referred to as Suga Momma). I have no clue who my biological father is. I am currently researching that subject, but we shall discuss that later in the book.

As ridiculous as this may come across, I do not know much about Lynn. The little that I do know is just negative from every aspect. I am not going to nor am I trying to bash her in any way. I am completely and forever grateful to her for:

1. Making the tough decision to continue the pregnancy and give birth to me and
2. Making the choice to allow my grandmother to formally adopt me.

I am sure that extenuating circumstances were a heavy influence. I have an older brother who had been removed from her custody by state officials. I was in the process of being removed from her custody and I also found out that she was in jail at some point while I was a small baby. As a mother myself, I cannot imagine my children being taken from me nor giving them away without a fight, however I do not know the path that she has had to walk. I just know that we manage our roles as mothers differently. I am not the same type of mother that my Suga Momma (adopted mother) was either. I am the best mother I can be to the children that are mine. Ever since I was a small child, I have had this recurring dream of being a little girl in a courtroom standing between my adoptive parents before a judge. The judge asks me two questions, the first being "Do you want this lady to be your mother?" I happily shake my head and quietly say "yes" and then the judge will ask me "Do you want this man to be your father?" and boom, I wake up. It never fails. No matter how often I have that dream, I wake up at the same point. At an early age, I found out the hard way that the dream is a repressed memory. At the age of 4 or 5, Sugar Momma and Paw Paw (my maternal grandmother and step-grandfather) formally adopted me.

For most people, this is an amazing time in life. Someone loved me enough to rescue me from the situation I was in to give me a better life that I would not have otherwise had. I even thought my life was perfect. I did not see the oddities that were my building blocks at the time. Older parents were not the "norm" in the 80's. The only odd memory I have is my mother telling me repeatedly that once I was "old enough" she had something "very important" to tell me. My mother wanted to tell me herself that I was adopted, and it should have happened that way. Sadly, life does not always work out like we plan. It has been my experience that some black families do not process the adoptive family dynamic properly. Especially in cases like mine... my adoption was intrafamilial. My maternal grandmother adopted me from her youngest biological daughter. Looking back, the transition was not the easiest or simplest for everyone involved. Part of the process of the adoption was formally changing my last name from Pennie to Griffin. By this time, I was in the first grade in school. In the middle of the school year, all my records had to be updated and my teachers had to learn my name all over again. It was also at this time in life I learned how disrespectful, messy, and inappropriate "adults" can and will be. My physical education teacher, who happened to be a former classmate with my birth mother, Lynn, decided one day to insert herself into our family business. This particular day she asked me, "Why did your grandmother change your name?"

I was about 6 or 7 at the time and my "grandmother" was the only mother I had known. Naturally, as any child at that age, I, being now irritated, inquired what was she talking about. She proceeds to tell me that my mother is not really my mother and that my sister is really the woman who gave birth to me. As you can probably imagine, I was completely devastated. Everything I had known in regard to my family dynamic, up to that point in life was a lie. I went home distraught. After my mother saw how upset I was, she of course asked me what was wrong. I recapped the day's events for her. My mother was livid. I became terrified thinking I had done something wrong. However, my mommy pulled me into her arms and reminded me that she had said on numerous occasions when the time was right, she had something to tell me. My mommy told me that what my teacher told me was true however, that truth did not and would not change our relationship. She consoled me with hugs and kisses and the declaration that she and my father had been there all my life and had treated me as their own and would continue to do so and that nobody could change that. I viewed life differently from that point on though. I learned that just because a person is of a certain age to be considered an adult, it does not mean that the person will have the wisdom to behave as an adult. I also realized that the way my mother raised me was different from other kids my age. I was not afforded certain luxuries and opportunities typical to my age group. I was expected to be seen and not heard unless I had something of value to say. While other kids played outside every day, I was reading all kinds of books and mastering the piano. I was taught that "God has his hand over my life" and that I needed to prepare myself and act accordingly to be a leader in Christ and the church. Growing up I attended church services almost every day and all day on Sundays. The beginnings of my relationship with God were a merger of "I just want to be a regular kid, God", "If God loves me so much then why is my life such a mess" and ".... because momma said so". I will address how that all ties in later.

People can be cruel. There is no changing that. What you can change is how you react to that cruelty and how you allow it to affect your spirit and circumstances. I had to deal with ridicule for being adopted; having an "old mother;" my own relatives being unsupportive and mean; the list goes on and on. I allowed that to make me bitter, but I also used all of that as motivation to achieve goals, even if that motive was to be better than the people causing me pain. Unbeknownst to me God was right there to whole time molding me, growing me and yes, protecting me. Even though I did not understand God completely at that age, my mother kept me in church, taught me how to pray and constantly reminded me of who God was to her. God used her to lay the foundation in my life to build my relationship with him. If I had not been adopted, I believe that I would not have received that foundation that my future required. It is also highly likely that my life would not have been remotely similar let alone the same to what it has been.

****

Let us address the proverbial elephant in the room, shall we? Lynn, my biological mother. In 2018 I published my first book, a novel entitled *Phoenix Rising.* For whatever reason, Lynn got it in her head that I had written a "tell all" that solely focused on her. *Insert eye roll here*. What I am about to say may seem outlandish, however it's reality: I barely know this woman! When I was a young girl, I found Lynn intriguing and mysterious. She dressed really flashy and was always on the latest trends. She was wearing sew-in weaves before it was the norm. I'll never forget the one day that she was visiting and her track had gotten loose and the complete shock that came across our mother's face when Lynn asked her to re-sew it for her. Keep in mind, our mother had to use a regular sewing needle and regular thread to complete this process. I, being a young girl was astonished at this sight. Laughter escapes me now as I share this moment with you. Lynn always had a different sponsor. By sponsor, I mean different men that financed her lifestyle. She was a stripper at some point, and she was exceptionally beautiful. Lynn was also very mean and manipulative. A huge part of me believes that the animosity that she directs at me is all stored resentment for our mother, Suga Momma. What's pathetic about it is the fact that she pretends to be oblivious to her ungratefulness. Which is why she's never said anything to our mother about it. How can a person pretend to be a victim when in reality, Lynn is just reaping the consequences of her own actions and decisions. Actions, that had already consumed my older brother and were quickly about to consume me had it not been for my grandmother adopting me and keeping me in the family. I have an older brother, who due to circumstances beyond his own control and yet, directly related to our birth mother's bad decision making, he ended up shot and permanently paralyzed. My big brother and I were not strangers, he came to visit us every summer however he lived full time at an assisted living facility in another city.

We were as close as can be expected considering the circumstances. When we were 9 and 15 years old respectively, our birth mother gave birth to another baby. He was the absolute cutest baby I had ever seen. I was instantly in love with him. My younger brother and I were close since we all lived in

Houston. I saw him a lot more than I saw my older brother. One day we were at my sister/aunt's house and the announcement was made that my older brother would be in town in a couple days. I was beyond excited to have both my brothers together. My young mind figured that maybe our bond would be closer if we were all together in one place. It was at that moment I was informed that not only would we not all spend time together but that my older brother did not even know we had a younger brother. I was told not to tell my older brother anything about our younger brother.

This. Blew. My. Mind!

I did not know how to process this information. I could not understand it, and nobody would explain it to me.

Years passed by and one day, my biological mother came over to our home and asked my mother would she allow me to go to a baseball game with her and my siblings. My sugar momma was reluctant and apprehensive however Lynn begged and stated that we would be there with my older brother who was in town with his school on a field trip. Reluctantly, Sugar Momma allowed me to go. I do not even recall what team the Astros were playing. I was completely excited that my siblings and I were all together finally. The only things I remember about that game is that it was the Astros, my oldest brother was utterly excited to meet our baby brother and that the Astros lost. It is weird how life works since approximately 3 months after that meeting, our next time together would be at our baby brother's funeral.

The first funeral I ever attended was that of my baby brother. He was 6 years old. Amazingly, I was more hurt for my oldest brother who barely knew Jason, as much as I was hurting over him being deceased. Death has surrounded me since that moment. I watched my cousin get shot in the head in front of me. A good friend of mine was killed in high school. Being surrounded by so much death at such early stages in life left me shell shocked in certain areas of life. Lynn decided to have our little brother cremated, which at the time made absolutely no sense to my young mind. However, later on it made perfect sense. I don't know what her specific reasons were, but I can imagine that finances had a lot to do with the situation since cremation is much cheaper than burial.

 Life was never the same for me after that. Eventually Lynn gave birth to another daughter. Lynn also got married for the first of many times, to my younger sister's father. Lynn and I have had a roller coaster of a situationship all my life. There was the year that I saved my allowance and bought all the ladies in my life cards for Mother's Day. Lynn told Sugar Momma that I was being messy. Needless to say, that I never did anything nice like that again for Lynn.

Lynn would also go out of her way to make sure that everyone who would listen, know that I am her biological child. Never mind that she has never raised me nor took care of me. I'm not sure if it was a rare occurrence back then but, I literally had a deadbeat birth mother that has never contributed to my life in a positive manner financially, mentally, or even emotionally for that matter. She's never supported any extra-curricular activities I participated in either. Lynn has never even been a source of positivity towards anyone that I know of. Yet occasionally, she would get a wild hair up her ass to want to play "mommy" to me. There came a point when I decided that I was no longer going to deal with her drama. I received a letter from her in the mail one day. In this letter, she wrote that she had "heard rumors" about me being "loose". She clearly had gotten me confused with herself. I showed the letter to my Sugar Momma, and we had a talk about it. She gave me great advice as always and she taught me a strong life lesson. People, especially relatives will more than likely be the meanest, nastiest people that you will have to deal with. You must learn to disregard what people say about you. This is why it is imperative that you are secure in your self-awareness and your character. No one should be able to make you question or doubt yourself.

When I was in high school, someone presented the bright idea to have family meetings. The premise of these family meetings was that we would all lay our issues on the table and then work toward a resolution. While this seemed like a great idea in theory, it didn't exactly work out like that. All that happened was old wounds were reopened anew and no resolution was on the horizon, because two things were missing: transparency and accountability.

At one of these meetings, I asked Lynn if she would finally tell me the name of my birth father. Since all my other siblings knew their fathers and had relationships with them, I just assumed she would tell me. She did not. Instead, she chose to lie and deflect. Years later I would come to the conclusion that I am the product of a one-night stand, or she lived a double life and just did not want to tell the truth.

****

Now here is the challenging part. I cannot only focus on all the great things about Sugar Momma. She was an amazing woman. I still learn about her, and her lessons still teach me, presently. My mother was also flawed. I feel she allowed Lynn to get away with too much. I also feel like she allowed the opinions of others to matter entirely too much sometimes. My main complaint was that she put way too much emphasis on finding the "right man". My mommy would go on tangents sometimes about this when all I wanted was support for my dreams and goals. I eventually came to terms with the fact that my momma, being born in 1934 and there was not much a woman could do on her own in her generation; just wanted the best for me as she knew it from her perspective. Looking back, I can acknowledge that she just wanted me to have her perception of a secure life. As a mother I can totally respect and appreciate that aspect. However, I just never wanted to be validated by a man. Before anyone takes this out of context, all I'm saying is that I am content and secure enough within myself that I am great and truly accomplished with or without a man by my side. I'm not the type of woman that feels incomplete if I am not in a relationship.

****

I have not seen nor spoken to Lynn since our mother's funeral in 2011. I have absolutely no respect for her as a mother. You would think that Lynn would have at least not been problematic considering her mother adopted me and raised me. Not once did my mother ever ask unstable Lynn for a penny to help with anything related me. There was no child support. She was never told not to come around or anything of that nature. Lynn, however, is still Lynn. When I published my first book *PHOENIX RISING* Lynn went on the offense and called my other siblings (aunts and uncle, biologically) and verbally attacked them as if they should have stopped me from writing a book. Lynn assumed my debut novel was about her (The nerve, right?) At this point in life, of my remaining biological siblings, I am the only one with children. She has never met or been around my daughters; and my sons, she has not seen since 2011. Until there is a genuine change in her, she will not have a relationship with my children. She is too toxic of a person.

On the flipside of that coin, I can respect Lynn as an individual. With the limited knowledge that I have of some of her circumstances in life, I can admire her tenacity and willingness to keep pushing. This woman was a young girl when her beloved father died unexpectedly, she's been arrested and in jail, she's had to bury her youngest child that died unexpectedly and very tragically, and lots of other tribulations. Yet, she is still living life on her terms and waking up each day to try again.

All in all, I am thankful that Lynn has been and is who she is. Why? I am a much better mother because I know exactly how NOT to be. I will not be the mother that manipulates and uses her children. God allowed my childhood to happen in this manner so that I can be the mother that my children need. My children will not have to recover from their childhoods as I did. My children do not have a toxic mother. I am not perfect. I do make mistakes. I also have no qualms about apologizing to my children when I have been wrong. Children are people. They have feelings, thoughts, good days, bad days etc. I am incredibly open and honest with my children as well, especially about topics they can easily do a google search about. You have to be transparent with your children. That is how the trust is built. No matter how uncomfortable the subject may be. Growing up the way that I did, also helped me to emphasize my children's bonds as siblings. I want them to always be close and have each other's backs as only they can. "We all we got" is what I drill into them. So that when they get older, they already have their inner circle. They will have spouses and all the other stuff, but their go-to people will always be each other.

I also appreciate the hustle ethic I obviously got from Lynn. As a little girl, I heard the stories and even witnessed her finesse men regularly. She was a beautiful woman. I believe my mother saw that in me and she helped me channel that energy into positivity. Not to say I have not used a man once or twice lol, it just was not my primary goal in life.

My mommy has been gone for ten years now and it still feels like just yesterday sometimes. I would give anything to even have one of our arguments, because at least she would be here to argue. Even though my mommy and I had vastly improved our relationship before she died, I still have some regrets that arise every now and then. I wish I would have learned to pick my battles sooner. I also learned that everything had to happen exactly as it was supposed to. I have the appreciation for her that I have because I know that I could have done better with the time we had. So, to all of you reading these words right now, that have a mother still alive and she's trying her best to meet you halfway in your relationship, here is my advice: Pick your battles. Sometimes, it is better to just say "Ok" and walk away. Keep in mind, that she's definitely allowed you to have the "win" instead of proving she was right.

So, my point is this, you can have a shitty childhood and your life can turn around. You just have to decide that you want to break the cycle. You do not have to be a product of your childhood nor your environment. Will it be easy? No. Nothing in life worth having is ever easy. Being pregnant is not always easy. Delivering or giving birth to a child is not easy. Nurturing your dreams and then doing the work to bring those dreams into fruition is not easy. Will it be worth it? Absolutely!

God allowed me to experience a lot of hurtful circumstance and situations. I could easily have decided to consume all the negativity and become bitter, angry, and vengeful. What does that solve, though? When and how have those adverse emotions ever churned out positive results? Unlike mathematics, two negatives do not make a positive in real life. However, in my case I chose to look at everything differently. If I wouldn't have been adopted, I would not have had a successful career as a musician. I have traveled lots of places and met some interesting people because of my talent. I have also been afforded the opportunity to live my life on my terms, which is something very important to me.

I probably wouldn't be a mother. Or if I was, it wouldn't be to the children I have now. Or I would probably be a completely terrible mother. There are many variables that could fit in this "what if".

In the big picture, I was able to accomplish a plethora of achievements that mean a lot to me like being a stay-at-home mom or being self-employed and being able to give opportunities to other people. We are blessed in order to bless others. So, If I had to do everything all over again, I wouldn't change anything. God has never taken something from me and not replaced what was taken with something better.

Even if you are reading this and your current situation seems hopeless, don't give up! God doesn't operate on *your* time however He's always *on* time.

Keep Ya Head Up...

"Cause I think we can make it, in fact, I'm sure
And if you fall, stand tall and comeback for more"

- Tupac Amaru Shakur

Growing up in the 80's with older parents had its ups and downs. Music was exploding and I am a music infused person. I love all kinds of music; country, rap, jazz, R&B, gospel, everything except for heavy metal, alternative and the likes. I mostly played classical and gospel music growing up and professionally because I was employed at Concord Missionary Baptist Church as a pianist, my mother didn't really allow me to listen to secular music often, but I would sneak and listen when she wasn't around and I'd get my dad to buy cassette tapes for me, but I mostly recorded songs off the radio. I'm pretty sure that if you're in a certain age bracket that you have no idea what I mean by "recorded songs off the radio". So let me explain, back in the day some stereos had the option to record on blank cassette tapes. So, what most people my age did was listen to the radio and wait for your favorite song to be played. Once the song came on you would press the record button and boom, instant mixtape. Basically, the precursor to "napster" or streaming services. The old saying, "Music soothes the savage beast" definitely applies to me. It doesn't matter if I'm playing the piano, making it myself or listening to the creation of others, I completely immerse myself into the music. The construction of it, is what draws me in. I can tell the difference between a quality made song and something that was just thrown together. Quality songs are like an onion. There are so many layers to it. It doesn't matter what genre of music it is. I didn't understand my yearning for music at the time, but it became fully understood later in my life.

Music ultimately became my safe space. When I was a little girl, somewhere between 6 & 8 years old, I would always go over to my Aunt Gloria's house as often as I was allowed since I was not allowed to go many places. It was the only place I could go at that time since my momma was so strict. I soon learned why she felt the way that she did.

One night, my cousin Mary and I were in her bed asleep when Tyrone, the younger of her two older brothers came into the room and placed himself on top of me. Tyrone began to fondle me and then Dexter, the oldest brother came in there and pulled Tyrone off of me and back into their room. I eventually went back to sleep but then I woke up with Tyrone back on top of me. This time he was giving his best effort to insert his dick inside of me. At that point, Aunt Gloria came bursting in the room, turned the lights on and snatched Tyrone off of me. My young mind, thinking that the situation was handled because:

1. I was where I was supposed to be.
2. I really did not understand what had just taken place.
3. Tyrone kept coming in a room he was not supposed to be in at that time of night.

The next thing I know is I got snatched up out of the bed and dragged to the kitchen and was told I was getting a whipping. I was chased around the kitchen table a few times before Aunt Gloria caught me and whipped me with a belt. I never told my mother because as a child I thought I had done something wrong, and I did not want another whipping. Later on in life, I just realized that some people would justify the wrongs of others simply because they do not like you and your presence brings to light things that they desperately try to keep hidden.

Years after Tyrone had been in prison for unrelated convictions, I asked Aunt Gloria why she only whipped me and why did she whip me at all. She got angry and denied the entire situation. Needless to say, I learned about a lot at an early age. I did not know before that incident that boys and girls had different anatomy. I also no longer had a clear distinction between right and wrong. I never spent the night at Aunt Gloria's house after that incident and my momma who was elated never questioned why. I would not realize at that time how that situation had affected me until years later.

It would be safe to say that I have always been very resilient on the surface. I was not closed off socially after I was molested, and I was not withdrawn, emotionally nor socially. I do recall becoming very sarcastic and snarky though. The feistiness that is prominent in my personality began to shine through at that point. Looking back, I can now recognize those behaviors as a defense and coping mechanism. I always knew that my situation was wrong and so was Aunt Gloria's response I just could not justify why I knew it was wrong. I also learned to speak up for myself after that. As the years passed by, I formed the belief that Aunt Gloria just flat out disliked me. It was my belief that she despised me for circumstances beyond my control. Instead of directing her energy towards our mother, she decided to take her frustrations out on me. Don't get me wrong, she would try her best to hide it, but her true feelings were always revealed during critical and/or traumatic moments.

****

The night of my son's funeral in 2004, I was raped by someone I thought I knew very well and trusted. After the funeral, my ex-boyfriend Jerome called me and asked if I wanted to get out of the house. I happened to be at my older cousin's apartment at the time because it hurt too much to be at home. Jerome picked me up and we went to meet some of his friends at a restaurant. I do not remember much because I consumed an insanely, ridiculous amount of alcohol that night. I was completely withdrawn and numb. I interacted with the people at the table but for the most part I was reserved. I thought I could trust Jerome because he had always given me the impression of being protective of me. The last thing I remember about the restaurant was that I was practically carried out of it to the car. There were two people, one on either side of me. Right before getting into Jerome's car, I vomited all over one of the person's feet. I blacked out after that. When I woke up, there was a guy between my legs and Jerome was next to me. I tried to pull away and Jerome was like "whoa, no, hold up" then I said no. Then I vomited again and passed out again. When I woke up again, I was naked and, in the bed, alone. I never told a soul until now. Contrary to popular belief, it is not easy to walk into a police station and tell a story that you do not have all the details to. I also believe that because of how my first sexual assault was carried out that I handled this situation in a similar manner. At that time, I believed that I held some accountability in that situation. I think because I received punishment as a little girl after being molested, because I was not believed then, I thought subconsciously that I would not be believed about the rape either. It took lots of therapy for me to realize that another person's lack of morals is not my responsibility. I am not a victim. I am a survivor. I did however become more cautious about who I surround myself with and I also became an advocate for others that didn't have the confidence to defend themselves. I stopped considering another person's feelings above my own.

I have not quite figured out all of the reasons that God allowed this, however one positive is that I emphasize to my sons especially, but also to my daughter that no means no. That is it. Once my boys get old enough to discuss the nuances of sex then

I will further emphasize that no is definitely no in every dating situation.

We have to release the self-induced guilt that some of us survivors end up with. I know I carried it for an exceedingly long time. I was also really angry. Do not allow yourself to carry the burden of other people's lack of morals and decency. Also, PLEASE TELL SOMEONE! Do not carry that burden alone. I made that mistake. It's an agonizing tether. If you do not feel comfortable telling someone in your circle, then tell a stranger, tell the police, and then get a new circle. Your circle or village should believe you in a crisis. I prayed for a better circle, and I now have a better circle. When Jerome returned me to my cousin's home, she went on a raged tangent and promptly kicked me out of her apartment because, as she put it, I "can go be a hoe somewhere other than her house".

As I write this, my heart is heavy because I know that the current climate consists of a specific sect of males aggressively attacking black women. I know that the general consensus of most black women is that we do not feel safe or protected with some of our male counterparts. I refuse to give into that and accept it as "it is what it is". I believe that as long as we women continue to speak up and make ourselves heard that the dynamic can and will change. Hope is an immensely powerful tool. Use it regularly as motivation to do the work so change can happen.

****

Because of Aunt Gloria's actions and how she treated me after her son sexually assaulted me, I did not handle my rape the way I should have. However, I use both situations for growth and for motivation to teach all of my children better. I am very candid with them, and I regularly have open conversations so that they can know that they can talk to me about whatever and whomever without fear of not being believed.

After I became a mother and my sons grew to an older age, I began to view Aunt Gloria's actions differently. I've come to the realization that some people are similar to Tom Cruise's character in *A Few Good Men* when Jack Nicholas's character told him "You can't handle the truth!" Even though she saw with her own eyes what her son was doing, she didn't want to accept it. Honestly, what mother would? It is definitely a hard pill to swallow when our children exhibit behavior that goes against everything, we have taught them. My children haven't done anything that egregious, however I was hurt the first time I caught my son in a lie.

Most recently when our brother died, Aunt Gloria showed me who she was again. This time, I had the fortitude to stand up for myself and pause the relationship. I handled the situation in a way that should have been addressed years ago. I wished her the best and I harbor no ill will. I told her that I will always love her... from far, far away. As I told her, we've come to the end of the road, and I will not allow her to continue to run rampant in my life. About 6 months later, following my return from out of town, we as women were able to have a much-needed heart to heart conversation. Now, our bond is strong. She no longer views me as the spoiled, entitled brat and I no longer view her as malicious.

What I have ultimately learned from my relationship with Aunt Gloria is this: we as people sometimes just lack accountability. It is very much so possible for a person to have the best of intentions and drop the ball. Aunt Gloria is a very loving and endearing woman. I don't know the loads that she has had to carry in her lifetime from her perspective. I don't want to leave the wrong impression; Aunt Gloria is a big part of my village, in regard to raising my children and being supportive. She is giving, loving, and very much loved by me, my children and all that know her. I have realized that, as I did with my mother, I pick and choose my "battles" with Aunt Gloria. People are not required to be accountable on my or your timetable. It will only happen once that person is willing to look within and do the work. It becomes a form of judgement when you expect others to operate within your predetermined parameters.

****

Christmas Day 2019, I was 9 months pregnant and due any day. I arrived at my dad's home with my three children and very tired. Something felt very off in my spirit. As we were getting out of the car, my brother (who is now deceased) stumbled out of the house incoherently drunk. We got into a very heated argument that almost became physical. My children were understandably upset. Now, the problem with this incident is that my kids had not seen my brother at that level of intoxication. I would always try to protect my brother's image in their eyes. I couldn't protect either party in this situation. A few days later after I calmed down, and gave birth to my youngest child, I allowed the kids to call my brother and express their feelings. It was complicated for all of us. However, we did get past it and thankfully, there weren't any more incidents prior to his death. We were able to mend the relationship.

Here is what people fail to realize: I can wish the best for you and not be around you. Forgiveness is NOT synonymous with relationship. I will not forget what was done. I can and will forgive, however, my space is precious and if any person can't respect that, then that person will not have the privilege of my space. The reverse is true as well. If I am not productive and positive energy in a person's life, please tell me and I will either make the necessary adjustments or I will remove myself. Likewise, that person does not even have to inform me. If I am the toxic person in someone's life, they have the right to remove me without an explanation. Protect your spirit, people! For generations we have allowed people in certain categories like relative, friend, elder etc. to give others a "pass" when in reference to how they treat us. Titles don't mean anything to me. Father, mother, sister, brother, cousin, young, or old. If that person is not behaving in the manner, you believe describes that title in your life, then bring it to that person's attention. If the behavior ends, then you know the relationship is worth salvaging and fighting for. If, however, the person does not change their behavior then remove that person from your space. Your self-care is way too vital and should be maintained at all times. There's an old saying: How can you pour into others if your cup is empty? This statement simply means that, you can't give the very best version of yourself to others until you are completely whole and healed. If you are thirsty, would you pick up an empty bottle or a full bottle of water to quench your thirst? The same applies to being a great leader, friend, parent, sibling, etc.

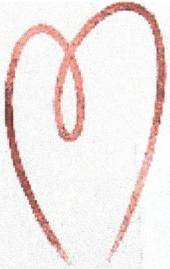

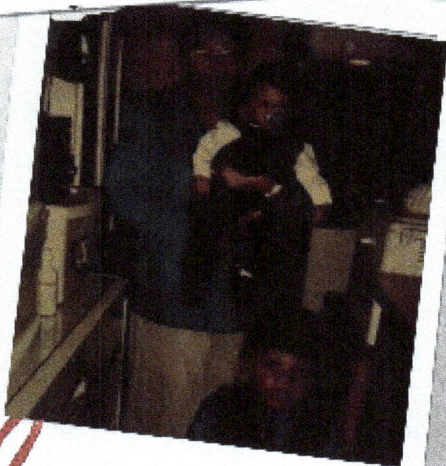

Never Had a Friend Like Me

"Who can I call when they all fail
Collect calls to my Dawgz from the County Jail
Sendin' me mail"

- Tupac Amaru Shakur

I am terrible at relationships that aren't centered around my children and my family. It does not matter if it is friendship or dating. I was raised as an only child so, between that dynamic and not being taught how to "be a friend" when certain circumstances arose, I just wasn't prepared to be a friend early in life. I wasn't taught how to treat a guy in a romantic relationship. However, I'll address that later on. When I was in Elementary school, I thought my best friend was a girl that lived two houses over from me simply because she was the only person that my momma would allow me to hang out with.

When I was in middle school my best friend was Candy. We met under very messy circumstances.

There was this messy girl in my homeroom class that told Candy that I was talking trash about her, keep in mind, I had not ever exchanged so much as pleasantries with the girl in my homeroom class. So, one day at lunch, I was in line by myself and Candy, the messy girl and some more girls approached me while I was standing in line. Candy asked me about the accusations the girl made and me being the social virgin I was had no idea what she was talking about. I said as much to Candy and we both quickly realized that the girl really did not like me for some unknown reason and wanted someone to beat me up. Well Candy and I were raised by older mothers, unbeknownst to us at the time and so we were taught not to let people stick keys in our backs for their entertainment. The messy girl ended up getting her ass kicked and Candy and I became best friends. Even after she left the school, we remained close. Our friendship faded away around the year 2005 for no reason specifically. I was in a different space at that time and so was she. My mother was fond of Candy which is more than likely why I clung to our friendship initially and after the death of my son and another situation, I just shut down. I didn't feel safe emotionally with any person that had been in my life around that time.

In high school, I spent my freshman year at Waltrip. I would get to school super early because my momma worked at the school. One morning, I was sitting out front like I usually did, and a student arrived early as well, walked up to me, and introduced herself to me as Marcy. She seemed like a really cool chick. Marcy was a couple grades ahead of me though. We eventually became really close, or so I believed. My experience with "Upper classmen" was limited to what I saw on tv. I was an introvert and socially awkward in a quiet way. Up until high school, I dealt with extreme colorism and insecurity issues with other girls in school. The whole routine of "She thinks she's cute because she's light skinned with good hair" was a five-day weekly occurrence. I always had my head held high and was very self-confident. My mommy instilled lots of self-esteem boosters into my life. So when I formed a friendship with Marcy and she would give the appearance of being concerned about me in regard to the boy I was involved with at the school, I believed she was being a genuine friend. When that young man and I went through our breakup, I thought she was being a supportive friend when she became as angry as I was. The guy had embarrassed me in front of a large group of students and faculty. However, I eventually fell back from being around her when all of a sudden, she and my ex had become the best of friends. I found it very weird that two people who allegedly didn't like each other and had negative things to say about each other, were suddenly joking regularly. Years later on in life, it would be those same shady actions again, except this time it wasn't a high school boyfriend it was my son's father. It just made me realize that the friendship just was not genuine. When we would go out to the club, she would always change clothes once I arrived at her house. There was also the time, a couple of guys were eyeing us in the club, and she decided which of us was going to talk to them in a specific setup. So, when the guy she selected for herself came up to me, Marcy read me the riot act when we got in the car that night as if I had somehow wronged her. What was I supposed to say to the guy? Was I supposed to tell him that I can't talk to him because my friend saw him first and she decided that you should talk to her? At the end of the night, we were invited to breakfast, and she insisted that we accept the invitation. I never told her that I gave the guy a wrong number because

1. I believed it was the right thing to do as a friend

2. I was not interested in him

Marcy was the type that had to meet someone every time we went out. I am not. More often than not, I preferred to be left alone.

I will say this though. When I went to jail, she did write letters while I was there, and she sent money. When I was released, she had a plane ticket at the airport waiting for me. This is not the sum total of our friendship, only the major parts. There were good times as well. In this case when it was bad the infractions were major. This created an imbalance in my belief.

At the end of my freshman year, I transferred to Barbara Jordan high school, where I met Nancy. I thought my best friend was Nancy. Nancy and I met because we had 90% of our classes together. At that time, I was not a social butterfly however, since I saw her for much of my day, I struck up a conversation by introducing myself. I won't say we became friends immediately but we did become close or so I thought. Looking back, I was desperate for a friend my age. My momma never explained to me that I should never be desperate for friendship. She only emphasized not being desperate for a man's presence. Eventually, Nancy began to try to tear me down verbally. I never said anything. As I am writing this manuscript, I still cannot answer why I never told her about herself, lol. She would say slick stuff like I should not be so loose, yet she was dating two different guys at the same time, albeit at different schools. Nancy's mom and my Aunt Gloria had been acquaintances when they were younger, so eventually my mother allowed me to spend the night at Nancy's house or to go to parties with Nancy. So that went on well into our junior year. Nancy left Barbara Jordan shortly into our junior year and transferred to another school. We kept in contact but of course, it was not the same. So fast forward to September 2000 and we've both graduated from high school. Nancy has gone on to college and I had to drop out because I found out I was pregnant. Since I only vaguely remember the details of how we ended up hanging out this particular day, I will just address what happened. I was 8 ½ months pregnant and Nancy came to pick me up to ride with her to visit her guy friend. Well, we were at a red light and there was a truck in front of her. She started refreshing her makeup and when the light turned green, Nancy pressed the accelerator and drove into the truck in front of us that had not moved yet. The air bags released and hit my stomach. The impact did not seem that intense, but I guess because it was a close impact it made a difference. So, the driver of the other vehicle did not make a big deal out of it since his truck was raggedy to begin with. The problem was we were in Nancy's mother's car. While there was no damage to the outside of her vehicle, the airbags told everything. Now by the time she was done negotiating with the other driver, I was starting to feel different. Nancy did not even bother to ask if I was ok. She proceeded to go straight to the dude house anyway since we were so close. The only repercussions she seemed concerned about was dealing with her mother's anger about the accident. I went into labor a few days later. We would talk sparingly after that since I had reunited with my son's father, and they too did not like each other.

So, in 2004 when my son died unexpectedly, I called her because as weird as it sounds, she was still the only person that I felt I could express my hurt to. While I love my mom dearly, at that moment in life, I did not want to hear scriptures and prayers. Nancy was not available. I found out the hard way that Nancy was not my friend. Prior to my son's death I had heard rumors that she had spoken negatively about me to mutual acquaintances of ours. I am the type of person that I have to see or experience something for myself to believe it. Nancy did not call to check on me. I always called her during that time. So, when the day of my son's funeral arrived, I was a robot operating on auto pilot. We were at the church for the repast, and I just remember Nancy coming up to me saying she had yet another someone, some guy for me to meet. She then asked me to walk her outside to see her off.

Some months after that, Nancy sent me an invitation to her wedding. That was the straw that broke the camel's back. I realized in that moment that Nancy was not my friend and never would be. I sent her an email instead of an RSVP and told her that I was done with this façade of a friendship and that I would do us the favor of addressing it so neither of us had to pretend anymore. I do not recall receiving a response from her. Some years later, a mutual associate between us had a party to celebrate leaving Texas for a new career. Nancy approached me at that party and asked if we could talk. She asked what happened between us. Long story short, she said that she mishandled that time in my life and she apologized but stated that we were kids (we were 21 when my son died) at the time and she didn't know how to handle that then. I accepted her words. I appreciated the effort that she did not have to put forth. However, I dismissed it as bs. Why? Because it doesn't matter if you have experience with a particular type of relationship to the death. Death is death. And if you genuinely care for a person dealing with a loss, you make an effort to be there for that person. To be perfectly frank, I believe she just didn't want to be viewed at the type of person to claim friendship and not be there for the person in that situation.

****

I think that the worst of all for me was Tracy. Tracy is the sister of my ex. She taught me the hard lesson that she was only my sister as long as I was in a relationship with her brother. Plus, she always tried to compete with me in being a mother to my son. On the day, my son died, I was supposed to be the last person to see him in his hospital bed. She persuaded the staff somehow to allow her inside the room or knowing her type of personality she just walked in without permission. I was not able to kiss my sweet baby on his cheeks because his face was covered by the ventilator and attachments. I was extremely upset by that. She bragged about removing the attachment, so she was able to kiss him on the face. I never looked at her the same after that. Our relationship deteriorated drastically after that revelation. A part of me still has not forgiven her and I don't think I ever will. There were other instances but that is the most egregious.

I have no malice in my heart for Nancy, Marcy, or any of the other ladies that I have mistakenly labeled as friend. I had to experience those situations to learn that I was not as good of a friend that I thought I was. I know this now because I was blessed with an amazing friend. Monique taught me how to be a friend. I am forever grateful for her being placed into my life to teach me about friendship and sisterhood. I also would not appreciate the friendship that we have if I would not have experienced everything else.

Around the time that I was dealing with my legal situation, I found social media to be a welcome distraction. At that time, twitter was my preferred platform. Eventually I began to receive invites from people to hang out in real life. Coming from the generation that I did, it was weird to me initially. My curiosity as usual, got the best of me and I accepted an invitation to late lunch with some other women who seemed to be on top of their game. One young lady in particular seemed to have much in common with me and we clicked. I'll call her Sarah. Now me being the skeptical person that I am when it comes to allowing people into my space I had to "test" her. One day, she posted about being a resume guru and she gave the impression that she wanted to put people in positions to start a new career. At the time, I was still a freelance musician. I took that as the perfect opportunity to put my test plan in place. I reached out to her about her offer and the end result was mediocre at best from delivery to presentation. So, since I had learned from my previous friendships, I kept this young lady at arm's length. Now, after some years had passed and she was still in contact, I began to relax on my boundaries. I subconsciously was still holding on to the notion that if a person has been around for a certain number of years that it means something. Shortly after I gave birth to my youngest child, Sarah confessed that she had been discussing me behind my back with other people that claimed to know me and didn't. Sarah only told me this because she and one of the ladies she had been gossiping with had a disagreement and that person spread a lot of Sarah's business on social media. Now I should have terminated our interactions at that precise moment, but I didn't. Because she was forthcoming with this information, I decided to give her a second chance. She did the same thing again. I brought the situation to her attention and Sarah blocked me

In all of those situations, I was the common denominator. I had to take a look in the mirror and acknowledge and accept that I am flawed. I had to make the decision to improve and work on me. You cannot expect to receive something that you are not giving out. It's easy to look back and say this person did this and that to me, however it's not so easy to pick up a mirror and say well I've done this, this, and that to that person. I am transparent enough to say that with Marcy, I was superficial at best. I would only call her to hang out when I was bored. I didn't share my life with her. Hell, she thought I depended on men and my parents to pay my bills since I didn't share menial details like how I made a living. Or with Nancy, how I would always dump my issues on her however I can't recall if I ever reciprocated being a shoulder for her.

I am no longer desperate for friendship or any relationship for that matter. I love me as I am and accept myself for who I am. Free yourself to embrace who you are and make it mandatory to be accepted as you are. "As you are" is not a license to be a shitty person by the way. So, don't think that you can be shitty, and people will deal with you in that manner. Here is the thing, I have learned the value of the word "friend". I do not use that word so loosely anymore. I put people in the category that they belong in within my life and operate from that point. I also no longer engage in artificial situations. If I believe that a person is being disingenuous then I will remove myself from that person and the association. Life is way too short, to deal with anyone who is not reciprocating what you are giving out. Do not settle in amorous relationships and do not settle in platonic friendships either.

One Day....

"Man if you got kids
Show 'em you love 'em 'cause God just might call
'em home
'Cause one day they're here
And baby the next day they're gone"

- Chad Lamont Butler

RIP Pimp C

March 8, 2001 was the absolute greatest day of my life at that time. It was the day I first became a mother. I gave birth to a baby boy that I named Sencire Vysean. He was a handsome and had eyes like a cat. His eyes were bluish grey when he was first born and then changed to greenish brown. At the time he was born, his father and I were not together. So, I was shocked when he showed up to the hospital to see him. His father is who gave him the nickname of Poncho Sanchez.

Yes, his father gave him a whole name for a nickname lol, I tried my best to not give into that but obviously he won lol. Poncho was the sweetest and smartest kid I had ever been around. Motherhood came naturally to me or so I thought. Looking back, I was a terrible mother in my opinion. Not terrible in a negligent way or anything like that. In retrospect, I did not handle parenting as seriously as I should have. Thankfully, I had a huge village to help me out. I was the type of mother that would dress my son in all white and take him to a child's birthday party and expect him to not get dirty. Insane right? I, along with his father also allowed our son to visit with our relatives more than he was home with us. Even though our son would be with either of our parents, we should have spent more time with our child than they did. I know, I can only shake my head at my actions back then. The first few months were challenging because, I wanted to parent my own way and my mommy was not having it. Since I was still living with her, she wanted me to parent her way. I refused to do that. It wasn't that I questioned her knowledge, it's simply because she raised me to think and figure out things for myself so why try to prevent me from doing that?

So, when my son was 6 months old, I moved out into my own apartment. It's weird because the day that I moved out was September 11, 2001. I was on the phone with AT&T setting up my home phone account when the towers were hit. Things with my mommy eventually got better because I was now living on my own. So, a couple years go by and once again, Eric and I are at odds. So, on the weekend of January 25, 2004, I decided that I was going on a date. However, as I was getting ready to leave Poncho came running up to me and wrapped himself around my legs and he would not let go. Up until that point Poncho had never done that with me. He would be quick to tell me bye anytime I left his presence whether it was to leave the room or when dropping him off to my mother for her visits. However, this particular day he started crying and begging me not to leave him, I cancelled my date and stayed home with him. The next day was a Sunday and I woke up late for church, which was also where

I worked as a musician. I decided to leave Poncho at home with my dad and my brother since I would not be gone long. My dad and Poncho drove me to church and as I was getting out of the car, Poncho started screaming for me to take him with me. Long story short and due to legal ramifications, that was my last moment with him alive. The next time I saw him would be at Memorial Hermann Hospital Northwest. I would be told that I had to decide to remove him from life support and that decision ruined me for the rest of my life. I never quite looked at life the same after that. Having to make a decision of that magnitude at the age of 21 is without a doubt the most devastating experience I have had to endure. Even though the doctors informed me that there was no brain activity which meant that my son was deceased already, the decision was and will forever be brutal to carry.

****

I now have four children that mean everything to me. It took the birth of my youngest child for me to clearly understand the biblical story of Job. For those of you that do not know, Job was a righteous man in God's eyes and one day while Satan was lurking around looking for trouble, God asked him if he had considered Job. Basically, what happened was, Satan asked for God's permission to destroy Job's life and God allowed him to do everything he wanted except for tampering with his soul and his capability to live. In the midst of all he went through, Job never lost faith in God. Once his trials were over, God blessed Job with double everything he lost including his children. For a long time, I thought it was instantaneous like magic, how Job received his blessings. On the day I gave birth to my last child, I looked at her and began to cry because I realized that God allowed me to lose my first child, but he blessed me with 4 more children. It was not an overnight situation or instantaneous as my young mind once thought, nevertheless the blessings are here. I also take my role as a mother way more seriously, yet I also know how to stop and smell the roses and enjoy life with my children.

There are no boundaries to my protection either. My oldest child's father, unbeknownst to me was very abusive verbally, mentally, and physically. My child did not inform me until we were locked in the house due to hurricane Harvey. My heart broke because there was never any indication or clue that something was wrong. It also hurt because as a mother you don't want to believe that you've created a life with a person capable of such actions as well as accept responsibility for always allowing or encouraging your child to go be around an abuser just because the person has the title of parent. Needless to say, that I confronted the narcissistic individual about what my child told me, and he did not deny it and also did NOT apologize.

My child has not had any communication with the other parent since 2017. My child is better and so is our relationship. Just because a person portrays a certain image to others, that is what they want the world to believe. It definitely is discouraging that society will believe and defend these well cultivated images that abusers project. It works in some cases. In my situation, I had to learn to not defend my actions to people that it does not concern anyway. I had to learn to not give into the need to justify my actions or tell my side of the story. People are going to believe whatever they want to believe. You have to learn to not defend yourself and allow God and the truth to fight your battles. Now that I have learned that I will always do what is in the best interest of my babies.

Because, unlike majority of society, I know what it's like to have to bury your child and so this time around, I will do everything in my power to always do what's right for them FIRST and then myself.

Now, I am more than sure that some will read this and try to imply that I am bitter or that I am wrong for allowing the demise of the relationship. Let me clarify my stance. I will NEVER be ok with an adult addressing a child as a "bitch" in ANY context. Especially a "man" and I use the term loosely.

In my child's case, the other parent was calling him a "bitch" on a regular basis. He would also open hand slap my child in his face in public and private. So, I will be whatever anyone wants to call me. I sleep very well at night and so does my son. Initially, I had to rip off the scabs of my own wounds and have a heart to heart with my child. I had to push past my insecurities and open the door to my own demons to explain to my son that some people are just not deserving of your love. I then had to tell my son that everything he is experiencing with his "father", I too, experienced with my birth mother. I will not allow my son to chase after or feel as if he needs to chase after a narcissistic, uncaring adult.

I wasted a lot of my younger years trying to figure out what I had done to Lynn to cause her to treat me so disdainfully. I did nothing wrong. My child did nothing wrong. If the adult does not want to accept accountability for their actions, then by all means protect the child from that person. My mother didn't teach me that and she probably didn't realize how detrimental Lynn's actions were towards me; she probably did not know how to set boundaries for her daughter in our unique situation. Hell, she probably didn't know that you can remove people from your life without anger or malice in your heart. I am not my mother. It's all speculation in regard to my mother's thoughts and my birth mother. I know differently from my perspective and experience Please understand, a child IS NOT RESPONSIBLE for mending or nurturing relationships with adults. THE ADULT HOLDS THE RESPONSIBILITY.

My brother Prentice, who is biologically my uncle, passed away in March of 2020. I'm thankful that I had the opportunity to share with him how influential he has been in my life as well as how much he meant to me. My brother taught me how to drive a car. He taught me how to navigate directions (GPS wasn't around back then). He taught me a lot about life in general, however what means the most to me are two things:

1. Everything he taught me about the bible and God
2. How much he loved my kids

Before my brother and I began to have discussions about God, my beliefs were unrealistic due to what I was taught in the old school southern Baptist church I attended as a child. The church had me thinking and believing that God is this pious, untouchable, inaccessible, unreachable entity that judges for the sake of judging. Closely related to how most people are. What my brother taught me is that God is more like a very loving parent, without the human flaws. God is pure love. No irrational judgement. Disciplines with love and wants the absolute best for us. So, my challenge to you is to do the research for yourself. Don't only listen to what someone else has to say about God.

I would sometimes, remind my brother of everything he did for me and meant to me, and he would be shocked when new revelations popped up. I learned in those moments that he didn't do anything seeking future recognition and appreciation. He operated from a place of genuine love. The teaching moments in our relationship were just quality time moments for him. That's how we should be with each other. No ulterior motives... no judgments... just genuine love.

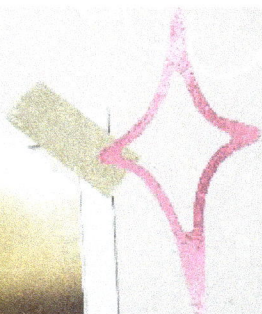

Peep The Picture...

"And it's deep cuz baby I can see us together

Cuz when it comes to you boo

it's whatever however

and I never

have to worry 'boutcha actin' a clown

cuz if I'm broke with no hope you gon' still stay

down"

- Slim Thug

In this chapter, I am going to address the three major relationships of my life. I had planned on only addressing one but since there is constant inquiry into why I feel the way I do in reference to relationships and why I try my best to avoid being in one, I decided to share my only three relationships. Yes, I've only been in three serious relationships in my life. There's an old saying that states a person will have three major loves in life: the first being puppy love, the second being the heartbreak and the third being the true love. I can attest that this is just an old wives' tale like most old sayings. However, I did learn a lot about myself from each one. So, let's dive in, shall we?

The Beginning:

Eric

I was a sophomore at Barbara Jordan, and I was the "girlfriend" of another guy when I met Eric. I put girlfriend in quotation marks because Twin had more than one girlfriend at that time. He claimed people were being haters but one thing I learned early in life; multiple people can't tell the same lie. So, if there are multiple people telling me that he has other girlfriends then I decided not to take the situation too seriously. One day at lunch, my homegirl Tiesha was talking to Eric and another guy and she called me over and introduced us. I was not a fan of guys with light skin complexions, but he was very handsome. I guess since it's a whole new century I can admit, there was an instant connection. The arrogant part of me would say that the feelings were not mutual and that he was more into me than I was into him.

Realistically, I would say Eric refused to acknowledge his feelings toward me verbally since acknowledgement would make him responsible and at that age, I can't blame him. We were both young then, so being serious was not really on my radar either. I can admit now that he was numero uno. We started hanging out a lot and one day out of the blue, his sister called me to go shopping with her. Looking back, I can see I meant a lot to him since he had to give his sister my number for her to even call me, even though he constantly denied it. We had an unstable relationship from the very beginning. Once he graduated and I was still in high school, our relationship got even more convoluted. Back then, I'd told everyone that I wanted to go to prom alone, and I did. The truth is Eric refused to go. He contributed to my prom budget, and he did take me out of town for the weekend afterwards though. We went to

Breaux Bridge, La for the crawfish festival. His sister and her friends joined us as well as Eric's friends. After prom and shortly before I graduated, we started to drift apart. He denied it, but I believe we both started to see other people. Our separation didn't last long, since by the time the summer was over, I'd found out I was pregnant with our first child. This was not a fairy tale, however. There were no roses and happy, happy, joy, joy dances. Eric was not happy at all, and I was terrified.

I can't say that I immediately made the decision to not have an abortion. Not having or even considering an abortion was more an act of defiance on my part than anything else. I just recall being prompted to choose that path every time I informed someone of my pregnancy. The only people that didn't suggest that I get an abortion were my parents and my brother. Their support was a huge influence on my decision to keep my baby. Although, I had no intention of being a burden on my parents with my new baby, it felt great that my parents fully supported me and had my back.

Although we had a rocky start, Eric and I eventually got on track and became the family that our son needed and deserved. Tragedy would eventually erode the already thin ice we were on. I can't say that Eric is the sole bad guy in our relationship nor the demise of it. I played a part in the destruction of our relationship. What amazes me is that, while he has done other hurtful shit, to my knowledge he has never thrown me under the bus by telling people about my indiscretions.

After we became parents and moved in together, reality hit us hard. Responsibility is not cute or fun when you aren't prepared or even want to carry it. So, there were infidelities on his part as well as mine. At this particular time in my life, I kept a journal.

Journaling has always been therapeutic; however, I should've had the good sense to keep it in my safe or at least a lock box. Anyway, one day I came home, and the bedroom had been destroyed. I was about to call 911 when I noticed a deathly still Eric seated on the bed with my journal in his hands. I was speechless. I mean, what does one say in a moment like that?

So, I just stood there, silently and waited for the proverbial sky to fall. When he finally looked up at me, initially I was slammed with a wave of guilt. I immediately, pushed the guilt to the side because as I said earlier, we both were guilty of cheating on each other. Eric didn't yell, he didn't throw anything, and he didn't even ask for any details to be repeated. Eric asked one question. He asked me if I wanted to stay together or end it. That's it. He told me not to answer him in that moment. He then got up and showered and went to sleep or pretended to anyway. After my initial shock wore off, I did the same.

****

Even though we eventually went our separate ways, I learned exactly how I wanted to be loved in a future relationship. I also learned that I would never cheat again. It was entirely too time consuming, dangerous, and draining. But I wanted to love and be loved as if I were capable of cheating and being forgiven. Eric never mentioned my infidelity after that day, and I never again mentioned his either. Most people will tell you that type of love only exists in marriage, but I beg to differ. I think you have to love on that level before you ever commit yourself to someone in that capacity.

The Illusion:

David

I always refer to him as my first "adult relationship" lol. Why? Because up until this point, I had not dated as an adult. Keep in mind that when I met David, it was a year later, following the death of my son and the demise of my high school sweetheart situation. David is a man's man, a gentleman, and he was also a real bad boy. He was protective and nurturing. Bad boy is not adequate to describe his past. However, he was also an entrepreneur. He taught me a lot about myself and about life. We met in the weirdest way. I was in my car on my way to pick up my BFF so we could go to the club. As I was about to exit the freeway, I lowered my visor mirror to put on my lip gloss. Unbeknownst to me, David saw me and decided to exit the freeway as well.

He followed me to the gas station and as I was inserting the nozzle into the gas tank, he pulled up on me. The man exuded confidence. His smile was perfect. Needless to say, he had my attention. Naturally, I gave him the impression that he was bothering me.

So, we exchanged a few pleasantries and cell numbers as well. While I accepted his number, I had no intention on calling him, ever. I was still recuperating, and I did not feel completely myself. One thing I learned from my relationship with Eric was to never be involved with another person when you aren't 100% in tune with yourself. Whether intentional or unintentional, my incompleteness was a doorway for emotional baggage and insecurities.

Well, life had different plans. David had called a couple of times and I would always brush him off. One day, about a month or so after we met, he called me and I decided to give in and meet him since other plans I had, cancelled. I don't recall where we were supposed to meet but we agreed on a specific time. I arrived at the location first and I called him to let him know. He said he wasn't there and that he would be there in five minutes. I literally watched the clock for five minutes and when he didn't call, I left. About 10 minutes after I left, he called to tell me he'd arrived. I told him that I had left already. He laughed; I assume he was amused. Due to his behavior following that day, I ascertained that he wasn't accustomed to women behaving that way with him. David went above and beyond to prioritize me into his life. It felt amazing for a man to be transparent about wanting my presence around him and not feel like an afterthought or just be there by default. If something needed to be handled, he took care of it without being asked or coerced. In turn, his actions inspired me to want to be better and be the woman who fit and elevated his life. Which just goes to show that even the worst of situations can have silver linings, you just have to look for them.

Our relationship was a whirlwind. After our second date we were practically inseparable. I tried to maintain my own separate life but if he wasn't working, he wanted me to be with him. Why wouldn't I want to be? We had fun together no matter what we were doing, and we discussed everything under the sun. Then maybe a few months into our relationship, the cracks began to reveal themselves. I woke up to him talking on the phone with his son's mother and he ended the conversation with "I love you" which wasn't initially odd to me but something in my intuition waved a huge red flag. Then other little things began to build up and from my perspective something was off. I in turn responded or reacted as I typically would. I started going out to the club with my girls regularly again. One particular night, when David was out of town, I met up with my brothers and cousins at a pool hall. Coincidentally, a guy that I previously met, happened to be there. So in between his games, he would come over to chat with me and he kept sending my drinks over to my group. As my family and I were getting ready to leave, David's voice came thru the speaker on my Nextel two-way. One thing he and I never did was start a two-way call without the alert first. I immediately thought something was wrong. So, as I stepped outside to take the call and to be able to hear him better, I learned that apparently a good friend of David's was also at that pool hall that night and he had given David a full play by play of the night's events. So, as I was trying to plead my case and defend myself from a couple of the untruths that had been inserted into the story, David decided to just terminate our relationship and disconnected the call.

I was hurt. I felt like my entire insides had been ripped out of my body. That was the longest month of my life. It took me a whole month to come out of the funk that I was in over that breakup. Once I did, I slowly started to piece my life back together. I didn't realize at the time that all I did was use David as a space-filler for the void that the death of my son had left in my life. Being with David gave me an avenue to be nurturing, loving and even in a twisted way motherly when his youngest son would be around since his youngest son was the same age my deceased son would have been. I've also learned that projection can be a drug. In my case, all the pent-up emotions that I carried were given an outlet which I thought was completely healthy at that time. However, I was only being used and was too blind to see it until it was too late.

Things changed drastically between David and me. So, instead of giving myself time to heal even after this traumatic event, I decided to completely immerse myself into school. School was an awesome distraction and slightly healthy as well. I say slightly because I still wasn't facing my issues directly. My momma was happy that I regained structure in my life and because I was doing something productive. David and I would still talk randomly but I wasn't feeling the same energy between us that was once there. Then I hit a financial rough place. I called David for assistance, and he readily agreed to give me the money I needed. When I met up with him to get the money, he then offered me another proposition. He offered to pay me to go out of town with him to re-up on his drug supply. The terms that were outlined were that there wouldn't be any drugs in the car on the way and that I would get half my money up front and the rest once we arrived back in Houston. I told him I would think about it. I had sold marijuana before, but cocaine was an entirely different situation altogether. There was a lot to consider. The risks were higher.

So, a couple days later, I was poised to tell him that my answer would be no when I was sideswiped on the freeway by an uninsured driver. My car was extremely damaged, and I did not have the coverage for my car to get fixed. Needless to say, that my answer of no was turned into a yes after that. So, we left the week before thanksgiving and ended up being pulled over in a small parish in Louisiana. Unbeknownst to me, there were drugs in the car and me being the loyal person that I am, I took the silent route. I didn't say a word to anyone after being arrested. I also naively believed that David would handle the situation. Ironically, that was the first and last time that I have ever been arrested. I found out a couple days after thanksgiving had passed that he left me there when he bonded out. We didn't speak again after that. He also never gave me the money that we agreed upon. I spent the next nine months inside a parish jail awaiting trial. After I finally bonded out, I would spend the next four years fighting for my freedom and my life. I would give birth to two of my children during these four years. I can't even explain the how or why behind my children being born during such a tumultuous time in my life. The trips back and forth to court were incredibly stressful physically during pregnancy. My trial began when they were two years old and two months old respectfully and it was pure torture. My two-year-old remained in Houston during my trial and my two-month-old was in the courtroom held by my god-sister in the audience since I was breastfeeding. When I was being questioned under oath in the stand, I'm sure that everyone thought my tears were because of the circumstances. My tears were in reality for what I was facing. My 2 yr old son was in Houston and my 2-month-old was sleeping in the audience and I was facing 30 years minimum if found guilty and I was afraid I would never hold either of my babies again.

* *

So, needless to say I didn't go to prison.

One day while I was still in the parish jail, the duty officer called my name over the loudspeaker. I was entering the ninth month of my stay and I just assumed I was being summoned to do some busy work since I had exhausted all options for trying to be released on bond. The next words that were spoken to me caused me to become frozen in place. The officer told me to roll up, which means to pack up my belongings because I was leaving. Now, in the days prior to this, a few people had been called to roll up, only to get to the front and find out that there was some type of mistake and be brought right back to the dorm. This is why I was frozen. I wasn't eligible for any of the typical bonds since I had no known ties to the state... I did but I don't involve other people in my shenanigans. I had resigned myself to believe that this was just a formality, and I would be back in my bunk in no time because clearly there was a major mistake. So, I packed up my belongings and informed my bunkmate to watch my locker until I returned. I didn't return. I was released on a PR (personal recognizance; free) bond and the next day I caught a flight back to Houston. I was aided by some people that I had met during my stay in the parish jail that I will not name out of the respect of what they did for me. If that isn't evidence of a divine presence, then I don't know what is. Here's something else to consider, I also didn't go to prison. I was facing 30 years and no possibility of parole the entire time. I was never offered a deal, which I probably would've never taken anyway because I'm stubborn and I also don't believe in paying for someone else's crimes. Once the judge released the jury for deliberation, the prosecutor approached my attorney with a proposition. He offered me five years prison with three suspended and credit for time served. That basically translated into an additional two weeks of parish jail time to complete the sentence. Although my attorney emphasized how "great" of a deal that was, I flat out refused to go back to being confined, especially now that I had children. I didn't care if it had been for two hours, I was not going back. I also realized that if the prosecutor was that desperate then that meant I had the upper hand. I doubled down and adamantly refused to do anymore jail time. Not only did they accept that but once I completed the probation period, I negotiated for an automatic expungement, which I also received. The jury never got to reach a decision since the agreed upon deal cancelled the proceedings and I went home to Houston that day without ever returning. So, as you can see, it's just more evidence of why I know without a shadow of doubt that Christ has been protecting and looking out for me.

The Fall:

Tony

I initially met Tony in 2001. I was standing in the driveway of my parent's home when he stopped his car in front of me. He got out of his car, approached me, and asked for my phone number. I declined. While he was handsome, at that time Eric and I were trying to work it out because our son was about two months old. At the time, I didn't realize that he'd given me a fake name. So, about a couple months later, some flowers were delivered to my parent's house and my mom called me to tell me about it. Mike had sent the flowers. I thought it was sweet, but I still didn't call him. About a year later, I ran into Tony again at a party. We did exchange numbers and he seemed interesting to talk to but something in my spirit wasn't right. I couldn't pinpoint what it was, but I did soon after that, find out. One day, while I was hanging out at my parent's house, I see Tony's car coming down the street. Tony had an incredibly significant and easily identifiable car. I found it odd that the car wasn't slowing down and once it passed by, I saw a woman driving and three small children in the backseat. My initial shock wore off quickly. I dismissed Tony after that. Tony had told me that he was single with no children and clearly that was a lie. I wouldn't see Tony again after that until after my son died. I believe it was about six months to a year later. He came over to my parent's house with flowers in hand to give his condolences. I thanked him and told him that while I was appreciative of his gesture, I didn't want to deal with anymore fake people. I can safely assume that Tony took my words as a personal challenge to prove me wrong in calling him fake.

About a month or so later, Tony began to shower me with gifts and attention. It was extremely overwhelming. I felt smothered. It's ironic how this same amount of attention I received from David didn't make me feel smothered. I know this was only because, I had already placed Tony into a certain box in my life and there was nothing that he could do or say to get out of it. He had already proven himself to be a liar and so there was no need for me to ever take him seriously.

Eventually he went to prison, and I moved on to a relationship with David. Once David and I broke up, Tony and I crossed paths again. This time, I was operating from a very hurt place. There was lots of resentment in my heart and Tony just happened to become the available recipient of all my toxicity. We began to date regularly, and he of course lavished me with lots of money, time, and other gifts. It was the only thing that kept him in my space. Tony would voluntarily lie about the simplest, strangest things. I would just laugh. I couldn't figure out why he felt the need to lie so much. For example, he called me up one day and asked if I would add him to my Nextel phone plan because he wanted us to be connected. He said that he wanted to prove to me that I should take him seriously about his requests to be my man. I laughed at that for a couple days. I added him to my plan though since he was already paying the bill.

Once I was arrested and began dealing with that whole process, Tony disappeared. I didn't hear from him nor see him for a couple years after that. By this time, I had a child. Tony claimed to be single and actually asked me to marry him. I refused; however, he wasn't deterred. He repeatedly told me after that moment that I would one day change my mind. He was right, after I gave birth to our child and he was locked up in prison, I gave in and married him. We got married on the cheesiest day that a couple can get married on, Valentine's Day, and I married him because whatever scam he had going on inside the facility allowed him to support me financially. Then, on the day before his release, my mother was rushed to the hospital. I picked him up the next day and drove straight back to the hospital, which is how my family found out I was married. Two days later, my mother died, and I caught Tony texting and chatting with a chick from his past. After my mother's funeral, I found out that I was pregnant again and I tried to make the marriage work. However, I got fed up really quick. There was so much to deal with,

1. It was my first time being pregnant without my mommy by my side.
2. Tony's mother is a very trashy, disgusting, messy woman.
3. Tony's side hoe was always chasing attention. She was beyond thirsty. Dehydrated is a better description for her.
4. Most importantly, Tony was so lost in his shenanigans that when he contracted an STD, the only reason he told me was because he thought he had given it to me. He hadn't realized that between all the drama, we hadn't had sex since before my mother's death.

That was the final straw for me. I filed for divorce immediately. When I went back a couple months later to turn in my final decree to finalize the divorce, I was knocked over by the revelation that not only had Tony went back on our original verbal divorce agreement, but he also filed paperwork to contest that he had rights to my property and inheritance. The proceedings would take a total of five years to complete. Tony kept going to prison during that time which caused the case to continually be reset.

****

I could go on with all the negativity that Tony caused in my life but what would be the point? At the end of it all as well as at the beginning, the primary cause for the entire situation is me. I allowed Tony into my life after I had already been given the confirmation that he was not a good person. I allowed bitterness from another failed relationship to steer me into this doomed marriage instead of finding the healing that I needed. I continued to hold on to this doomed situation because I didn't want to "lose". I had completely lost sight of myself. I went through so much mentally and emotionally because I subconsciously refused to let go of the familiar toxicity.

What I learned is this:

1. I stopped caring about what other people think about me.
2. I began to live life on my terms. As long as my conscience is clear, I can look at myself in the mirror, and I can sleep at night nothing and no one else matters.
3. I stopped chasing after people who don't chase after me.

It may sound cliché however its true. Before you can love anyone else, you have to first love YOU genuinely and wholeheartedly. This applies to children, parents, siblings, friends, and romantic relationships. You can also avoid relationships that waste your time because, when you love yourself truly, you won't tolerate being treated any kind of way by anyone. As much as we fight it, boundaries are necessary, healthy, and vital to life.

Daddy...

"Words can't express my boundless gratitude for you

I appreciate what you do

You've given me such security

No matter what mistakes I know you're there for me"

- Beyoncé

I was raised by an amazing man. My step-grandfather by birth and legally my father by adoption. We haven't always had the best relationship. My daddy would only attend certain functions to support me. He was at most of my piano recitals, and he attended certain church programs like, Easter and Christmas and maybe a few others in between. He wasn't the "show up" type. My daddy was more so a throw money at the situation type of man. If I wanted him to attend something or take me somewhere and he didn't want to, he would just give me a large sum of money and send me on my way. At first, this didn't bother me however, the older I got, the more it began to affect me. He could be extremely crass and inappropriate with sharing information with me. I can recall angering my mommy indirectly and unintentionally with my questions about something my daddy said or did. Then one day when I was a teenager, my daddy tried to make me choose between him and my mother in an argument and I finally put my foot down and told him that I was not going to be involved in their disagreements. That changed our relationship for at least a decade. My daddy wasn't as quick to do anything with me or for me anymore. I guess he felt betrayed. I felt used, I thought he shouldn't have put me in that position in the first place. No parent should ever put their child or children in a predicament to choose sides between their parents. It's immoral and extremely inconsiderate. Our relationship deteriorated so badly to a point that I didn't care if he would've died. My hero had become someone I didn't know, didn't like or love and didn't care about. That's a disgraceful place to be in.

When I purchased my house in 2016, I hosted thanksgiving brunch at my house that year. The dynamic between my father, brother and I had become so extremely tense. I had decided to let bygones be bygones. So, after thanksgiving, I took the initiative to start over from the beginning. I made the decision to re-learn my dad for who he is, flaws and all, accept that he's human, stop judging him and our relationship has since flourished. We don't have the petty arguments we once did. We started spending Sundays together as a family. My kids were happy and so was I. I had my daddy back. Something was still missing though. Then 2020 happened. Up until then, my big brother had been living with my dad because my dad is elderly. When my brother died unexpectedly in March, we all were at a loss. I think my daddy and I more so than everyone else. What most people don't know is that my first son, my mommy and now my brother have all died at my childhood home. I know that may seem eerie to some people but, it's a totally different situation to have to live in it. So, the day that my brother died, I rushed over to deal with that and as I was getting ready to leave, my daddy begged me not to leave him alone. It was as if no one else can understand or even remotely relate to what we have lived through. The very reasons that I have come to hate my childhood home are some of the very reasons that my daddy refuses to leave it. I begged him to but he's eighty-six years old and stubborn so, to appease him, I moved back in with him. It's challenging living in a home with so many happy memories and yet the worst memories at the same time. But how do you say no to your parent who's loved you all your life, put aside his own personal goals and adopted you so that you can have a better life?

****

In 2016, I actively began to search for my birth father. I had no clue where to begin and so I bought an AncestryDNA kit. I figured since this company had the most records and the most participants then something would have to click.

Let me backtrack... some years ago, back in 2009, I asked my birth mother one final time for information about my birth father. This woman has told me some of everything under the sun to avoid saying what had become obvious to me: she didn't know. The only truth that she ever mentioned was that he was from Oklahoma. I only believed this because my mommy cosigned this by telling me when I was much younger that "She went to Oklahoma and came back pregnant with you."

So, after about eight weeks my results came in and I was more confused than when I first began. I didn't stop to consider that relatives from both sides of my family would be in play. So, after reaching out to several of the matches with no response, I decided to take a break. At that point, all I was doing was making myself more and more frustrated. Being frustrated is not productive in any way. One night, I couldn't sleep so I started researching what one does after receiving these types of DNA results and as usual, there is a search for it. I located two promising groups; one is a search angel group, and the other is a Facebook support group. For those of you that are interested, I will place the contact information in the afterword section at the end of this book.

I reached out to the Facebook group first and here's why, I was leery of the other group because it is a Gmail message stream system that I still don't fully understand. After some time, my impatience got the best of me, and I sent my initial message to the Gmail group. A sweet woman by the name of Kitty reached out to me and walked me step by step through the process of how to separate out my maternal from my paternal matches. Kitty is known as a search angel and basically, she does most if not all of the work of locating relatives, for free. It took about a year and a half for us to narrow down the possibilities of my birth father, since my situation is a unique one. She gave me his information and asked that I wait for her confirmation before contacting him. There weren't a lot of possibilities on his side however, all of my matches on both sides were people unknown to me and she wanted to make sure that we had every match in the right category before moving forward. Lots of time passed and I began to think Kitty had forgotten me or joined me in my frustration with the whole situation. Then the COVID pandemic hit. I was certain that there would be no updates coming for at least another year. Then out of the blue, Kitty shocked me. She sent me an email that changed my life forever.

We now have confirmation that she had located my birth father.

I was in shock, disbelief, and scared all at the same time. Up until that very moment I hadn't thought about what I would do if I really found him. Honestly, I was subconsciously pessimistic. A part of me believed that I wouldn't find him. So, I responded how I always respond to fear... I took the next step, which was to write him a handwritten letter since email tends to give the appearance of a scam. I mailed it off and about two weeks later, I received a phone call from him, and we have talked every day since.

I've learned so much about myself in these few short months that now makes so much sense. It's mind boggling how I am so much like a person that I had yet to meet. We made preparations to meet face to face for thanksgiving of 2020 so by the time this book is released we will have met.

****

I can't say that I suffered any significant mental or emotional damage from not knowing my biological father all my life. I was raised by a wonderfully amazing man. Plus, I've always believed that you can't miss something that you never had to begin with. I'm just thankful that for whatever reason, at this juncture in my life, I am blessed to have two fathers that love me dearly. I'm thankful for the closure to the numerous unanswered questions that I had. This situation could have easily gone in a terrible direction but thanks to God, it didn't. My years of wondering and imagining are behind me and the future looks very bright. Not everyone has embraced this news with the same excitement that I have and that's to be expected. Regardless of what it is, don't ever expect for everyone to share in your joys. If you only have one or two people that celebrate with you then embrace it and appreciate it fully. You must also learn to accept that in some cases, you will be the only person celebrating you and that's okay also. Everyone isn't meant to go on every journey with you. A few of your journeys will be taken solo, so that you can take the opportunity to refresh, rejuvenate and reconnect with The Holy Spirit.

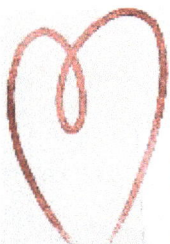

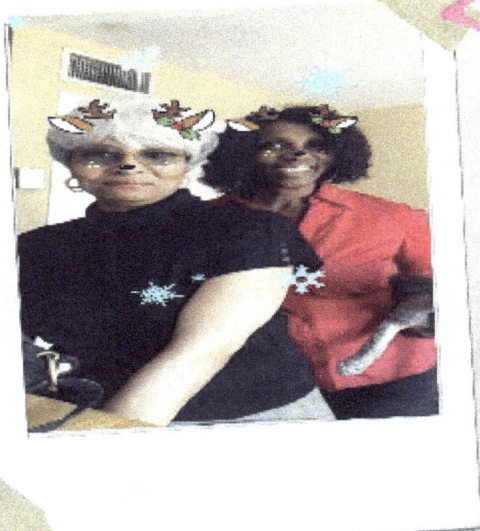

That's When You Blessed Me

"My life was torn beyond repair
I felt so alone, seemed no one cared
You came along, gave me a song
To ease the pain and erase the strain"

-   LA Mass Choir

My children are hands down, without question the absolute greatest blessings in my life. While my heart yearns for my first child and the possibilities that our lives could have been, I'm grateful now, just for the opportunity to have been his mother and for the blessing to be the mother to my present children. As a little girl, I didn't want the traditional things that most girls are conditioned to want: Husband, children, etc. The more that I would discuss those topics with playmates, the more I realized that I didn't want any of that stuff. I have a rebellious streak, as my mommy would call it. I don't want to have to check in and be accountable for another person. I didn't want to share myself or anything else. I didn't want to be tied down. Now that I've have the gift of motherhood, I cherish it. My children have healed me, taught, and teach me, keep me grounded and most importantly God used them to save my life. I was a hollow shell that was on a very self-destructive path. Now I don't ascribe that theory to a husband however, I'm completely glad that I decided to be a mother.

So, as I mentioned earlier, music has been a huge part of my life. I started taking piano lessons at the age of 3 years old. It's apparent that even at that point in life my path was ordained by God. The extraordinary woman that taught me how to hone my talent was Sarah Wooten. I still miss her, and it's been at least twenty years since she died. Mrs. Wooten wore her nails long, pointed, and fire engine red. She's the reason I can play the piano the same whether my nails are long or short. Some people struggle with that lol. When I turned 11 years old, Rev.

E.R. Green, the pastor of the Concord Missionary Baptist Church (the church that I attended as a young child) hired me as the musician for the Sunday School service. I was getting paid $100 per week. At that age, I thought I was balling. I was taught financial responsibility early since once I started being paid, I no longer received an allowance from my parents (Even though my daddy would still sneak money to me). I was put in charge of my personal frivolous expenses. There is a gift and a curse to generating an income at an early age. The upside is I learned financial responsibility and how to save and what purchases I really wanted vs what I didn't want to spend my money on. The bad is that I developed a slight sense of entitlement. I felt like I could do whatever I wanted to do since I was financing my own decisions. I remember when I purchased a two-way pager for myself (which was a silly purchase to make since I didn't know anyone else that had one at the time) but one day I got in trouble for something, and my mommy demanded my pager to take from me as part of my punishment. I was outraged. I actually said no. Yes, I actually told my mother "No" as a child. My stance was this: my pager wasn't hers to take since I bought it with my own money that I had earned on my own and it wasn't an allowance, it was my money generated exclusive of her. After she whooped my ass, (LOL) she reminded me that I was a child and that as long as I lived in her house as a minor, I would follow her instructions. I needed to learn that lesson because, now as a mother of children who are given large sums of money and other expensive items and they also generate their own income, I taught them to be financially responsible as well as to not lose sight of the reality that they are children still under my jurisdiction.

Getting back on track... I grew up in the southern Baptist church. I spent the years between age 11 and 18 in a bubble in regard to my church life. I believed that the people I considered "sisters" and "brothers" in Christ, genuinely loved, and cared for me. As long as I was viewed as a child, I was safe. Safe from the behind the scenes, back-office drama that goes on... Safe from the perverted sick, creepy men... Safe from the murderous tongues of the older women... That all changed when I turned 18.

When I turned 18, because I was a "leader" at the church, I was informed that I had to apologize to the entire congregation for "sinning". My egregious sin was getting pregnant out of wedlock. (Insert side eye and eye roll here lol) Later on, after I gave birth to my son, the slick talk and the lewd comments and jokes began to trickle out from some of the men at the church as well as other churches we fellowshipped with. I was no longer "innocent" I was now viewed as a woman that was sexual and accessible. My relationships with the older women changed drastically. They now viewed me as a threat or competition and not the "sweet girl" that was a sister or daughter.

I worked in the church circuit for over 20 years, dealing with the same behaviors regularly, until I began to feel burnt out. I wanted out. I no longer wanted to deal with that environment anymore. How was I supposed to just walk away from something that was a huge contribution to my life financially as well as socially?

I did what anyone should do when you begin to feel that way about a career. I began to pray about it regularly, and then I sat down and created a list of Pros and Cons.

As objectively as possible, I listed everything that impacted me the most positively, and negatively. After my list was complete, I began to formulate an exit strategy. As I moved closer and closer to my exit date, I began to have doubts. Doubts are normal and should be expected. However, I also paid close attention to the climate. The climate that I was in became increasingly hostile the closer I came to my exit date. I hope that I am not giving the impression that I wasn't afraid, because I absolutely was. Anytime I venture into the unknown, there is caution on my mind and intimidation. However, I thrive in these moments. I refuse to be bullied by a person and/ or a situation. Giving into fear is failure and I adamantly refuse to be a failure. I titled my first publication *Phoenix Rising* for a reason. That reason is because I interpret the bird as myself or anyone else who has been consumed by flames. The flames represent all that life throws at you that's meant to destroy you, all the people that tried to destroy you and just when you're down for the count, you are reborn stronger than before and able to accept and embrace the challenge. The race is not given to the swift, it's given to the one that endures.

I decided to follow my dreams no matter how intimidating it is. I've been peacefully happy ever since. You just cannot put a price on your peace. When I decided to write my first novel, I sought out a ghostwriter because, I didn't believe in myself enough to accomplish my goal on my own. I'm really thankful for the rejection that I received from the writers that I reached out to. Without that rejection, I would not have these accomplishments to be proud of. There is ALWAYS a blessing in rejection. Don't forget that. Yes, it is disappointing. Yes, sometimes it hurts like hell. Keep your eyes open and forward to be able to see the light at the end of the dark tunnel.

In The Midst Of It All...

"Through the pain and all of my sorrows
Through the tears and all my fears
The lord was there to keep me
For he's kept me in the midst of it all"

-   Yolanda Adams

Now that I've addressed the good and the bad...

Here's the UGLY TRUTH...

Following the death of my son, I became addicted to what we in Houston call "Drank". I also abused prescription pain pills once, but that purple stuff is what I always had to have. If I didn't want to drink alone, I would call Eric to buy the drug for me and we would literally sit in complete silence until we finished off the bottle. That process began to weigh heavily on me. I eventually found my own connect and began to drink alone. I don't remember how many Vicodin pills I had taken during my suicide attempt. My mother told me that she didn't even know I was at home because I had slept for so long. I thought I had died. What finally woke me up was a dream I had.

I vividly saw myself in the kitchen holding a butcher knife and after staring at my wrist for so long, I finally sliced it and bled out. I remember waking up screaming and covered in my own urine. My momma said that I scared the life out of her because she didn't know I was in the house. My mother also told me that I had to have been asleep for a whole day. I just know that I never took prescription pills ever again after that. I didn't stop abusing drank though. I was still hurting and self-medicating. I wasn't ready to face my life without my son. It hurt like hell.

What's weird is, people give me credit and props for being so "strong" and overcoming all that I have had to face. It's NOT me though. I can't take credit for any of my survival. My faith that held on by the bare threads in my subconscious had a lot to do with me coming out of the darkness. I just know that one day, I looked at myself in the mirror and this particular day is how I found out that mirrors are immensely powerful tools. If you look at yourself long enough, you will begin to see yourself beyond the physical and your spiritual side comes to the foreground. I began to see my scars, my soul looked burnt beyond recognition. I saw my physical flaws, as I had withered down to nothing. My eyes were sunken in, my hair was like dehydrated hay, and I looked like walking death. I cried like I had never cried before. I cried myself sick. After I vomited up what felt like my entire inside bodily organs, I dragged myself into the tub and turned on the water. As the water warmed up, I removed my clothing. I sat in the tub while the shower rained down and washed away all my guilt and transgressions. Then when I was done cleansing myself, I put on the biggest t-shirt I could find and forced myself to go outside. I sat in the sun and allowed the rays to re-energize me. I never consumed drank again after that day.

If I've given you the impression that I have it all together or that I prayed my way out of the dark hole I was in or if I gave the impression that I'm superhuman... I genuinely apologize. Yes, prayer was a major part of my process, however I can guarantee that it was my mother's prayers and probably some other people's prayers that were at work. I know and believe that God did the work however, I had to allow His spirit to filter into me. I had to be receptive to His love. I was not in a place that I wanted to pray to Him myself. I was beyond hurt. I was in tormented anguish. I also felt betrayed and abandoned because in my mind, I was thinking how can God be so loving and yet allow things like this to happen? Here's what I have learned. You cannot be so willing to accept all the great things that happen in life and at the same time believe that nothing challenging should ever happen to you. Let's be real, ok? If you have your arms wide open to embrace all the wonderful possibilities that come to fruition, then keep that same energy for life's downfalls and challenges.

I used to be one of those people that believed my actions do not have an impact on others around me. I learned the hard way that all my actions impact those around and adjacent to me. My actions affected my children, and they weren't even born when I made those decisions. Don't ever think that your actions and your decisions are yours solely. That's a lie. Every decision you make and action that you take will impact someone else, directly, or indirectly connected or disconnected to you. Don't ever allow yourself to think or believe you are alone in whatever challenge you're facing. YOU ARE NOT ALONE!

While you may be hesitant to open up to someone new or unknown to you, there is always someone for you to reach out to. Don't be afraid to try.

So, in closing, it is my prayer that you take the inspiration and hope that I found in the midst of these situations. I hope that you can look beyond the hurt and disappointments to see the silver lining, no matter how hard it may be to see sometimes. I pray that in those challenging moments when you just can't see your way, that you reach out for help. Sometimes we can be too close to a situation and can't see the entirety of it without assistance. Finally, it is my hope that you live your life outside of the boundaries. Dream beyond your limits. Allow your dreams to intimidate you. You deserve whatever you believe that you do!

Blessings… Love… Light

V.S. Griffin

"This time around I'm a make it clear
Spoke some things into the universe and they appeared
I say it's worth it, I won't say it's fair...."

- *Nipsey Hussle "Tha Great"*
    Victory Lap
    Rest In Power, King

AFTERWORD

FIRST, I WANT TO ACKNOWLEDGE AND THANK GOD FOR THE BLESSINGS TO BE ABLE TO BRING THIS PROJECT TO FRUITION.

About a month after the final edit of this manuscript was completed, I received some devastating news. The woman responsible for my entire writing career, had unexpectedly passed away. I am going through the typical mourning process; however, this just hits differently. Have you ever encountered someone so completely genuine? So refreshingly warm and empowering? I was blessed to have the opportunity to not only be friends with Cecilia but when I initially approached her with an idea for a book, she went a step further and became my mentor. The world was made better with her in it. She is loved… cherished… missed dearly. It pains me to not be able to share this finished work with her here. I will forever carry her spirit with me. Cecilia was more than just a profound woman; she was an experience. Her legacy will last forever. Until the end of my time, Fly high Yellow Bandit!

I also would like to thank Michel Roy for gracing this project with her energy in the Foreword.

For those that are searching for long lost relatives like me, I recommend my search angel, Kitty. I would not have found my birth father without her. She's absolutely amazing and if you would like to contact her, I've listed her information below.

Search Angel: Kitty@catspell.com

DNAgooglesearch group: dnaadoption@googlegroups.com

I want to thank my best and dear friend Sophie Scott for her efforts with the book. Sophie is a genius with styling and creativity.

A deep heartfelt thanks and lots of gratitude to Omar Auzenne of Auzenne Photography for his amazing talent for the book cover.

Instagram: @Auzennephotography

Facebook: facebook.com/auzennephotography

As always, I have to thank my children for their support on the days when "mommy had to work" … they are way more understanding than they should be for their ages. I'm truly blessed to be their mother. Sometimes, I feel very undeserving of the love they give me as a collective.

Finally, if you would like to keep up with what I'm doing or if you want to send a kind word, I've listed all my contact information below.

Facebook: facebook.com/AuthorVSGriffin

Instagram: Instagram.com/AuthorVSGriffin

Twitter: twitter.com/AuthorVSGriffin

Website: www.vsgriffin.com

On the Rox (mobile app)

Publisher: PGM, Inc

www.pgmincllc.com

Previous Works by the Author

Phoenix Rising

Self-Care Check Up Journal.

The Alphabet Trail in Color – Children's book

The Number Trail in Color – Children's book

You Are Somebody – Coloring Activities for all ages

The Color of Life – Coloring activities for kids